He, She and It

Summer People

Gone to Soldiers

Fly Away Home

Braided Lives (REPUBLISHED 2013)

Vida (REPUBLISHED 2011)

The High Cost of Living

Woman on the Edge of Time

Small Changes

Dance the Eagle to Sleep (REPUBLISHED 2012)

Going Down Fast

OTHER

The Cost of Lunch, Etc. (A COLLECTION OF SHORT STORIES)

Pesach for the Rest of Us

So You Want to Write: How to Master the Craft of Writing Fiction and Personal Narrative (WITH IRA WOOD), 1ST & 2ND EDITIONS

The Last White Class: A Play (WITH IRA WOOD)

Sleeping with Cats: A Memoir

Parti-Colored Blocks for a Quilt (ESSAYS)

Early Ripening: American Women's Poetry Now (ANTHOLOGY)

My Life, My Body (ESSAYS, POEMS)

On the Way Out, Turn Off the Light

On the Way Out, Turn Off the Light

Poems

MARGE PIERCY

ALFRED A. KNOPF   NEW YORK   2020

THIS IS A BORZOI BOOK
PUBLISHED BY ALFRED A. KNOPF

Copyright © 2020 by Marge Piercy

www.aaknopf.com

Library of Congress Cataloging-in-Publication Data

Names: Piercy, Marge, author.
Title: On the way out, turn off the light : poems / Marge Piercy.
Description: First edition. | New York : Alfred A. Knopf, 2020. |
Identifiers: LCCN 2020005033 (print) | LCCN 2020005034 (ebook) |
ISBN 9780593317938 (hardcover) | ISBN 9780593317945 (ebook)
Subjects: LCGFT: Poetry.
Classification: LCC PS3566.I4 O5 2020 (print) |
LCC PS3566.I4 (ebook) | DDC 811/.54—dc23
LC record available at https://lccn.loc.gov/2020005033
LC ebook record available at https://lccn.loc.gov/2020005034

Jacket photograph by Cyndi Monaghan / Moment / Getty Images
Jacket design by Jenny Carrow

Manufactured in Canada
First Edition

Contents

LANGUAGE HAS SHAPED MY LIFE

Language has shaped my life 3

Legacy of a vacant lot 4

The bike gave me wings 5

The air smelled dirty 6

Ambitious at fourteen 7

Late to find me 8

Images in oil 9

Save me 11

Argos, decades ago 13

The afterlife of old desires 15

At least a hill 16

Night's siren call 17

The depth waits 18

After the knee is replaced 19

Late fall, temperature 45 20

Doors opening, closing on us 21

Learning to be quiet 22

Being old at the end of the world 27

Even wine turns at last to vinegar 29

A reckoning in flesh 30

She is letting go now 31

Leftovers 33

What goes faster every time I turn around 35

Ultimate ultimatum 36

For your information—from your pharmacist 37

It diminishes 38

The longest lesson 39

Praise in spite of all 40

Taking stock in fall 42

A good death? 43

The sum of mortality 44

A profitable undeath 46

It still makes us happy 47

War of the old 48

Who can hold them, what can save them? 49

Joy to the world 50

U.S.

Dirge for my country 55

Way late December 2016 57

Consider these but you won't 58

Tyr marches on 60

U.S. 61

Their mouths are closed 62

Can't you hear them? 63

Illegal with only hope 65

Ladies who judge 66

Joiners 68

I can't write a love poem 69

Noon in a three-star restaurant 71

The President speaks 72

This is our legacy 73

Endless rage 74

The rain comes on like a tide 75

Another request comes in 76

Charleston massacre 78

Call to action 79

LOVE IS NO ACCIDENT

Am I pretty enough? 83

Much too early marriage 84

French lessons 85

Chicago one summer 86

The various flavors of argument 88

While it dies 89

Remnants of a dead marriage 90

Fooled again, she said 91

Time dims it 92

Where do pet names go in the end? 93

The cemetery of spent passions 94

That wild rush 95

No regrets 96

Let me never count the ways 97

Fire in winter 99

How we do it 100

Warm heart 101

Hairy nocturne 102

What happiness looks like 104

A litany of adoration 105

A JEW IN AMERICA NOW

The nonbeliever prays on Shabbat 109

Holy, holy 110

Hannah tells me stories 111

The wanderings of Hannah 113

In the Lodz ghetto 115

Holidays sweet and sour 117

The New Year of the Trees 119

We open ourselves too 120

Let all who are hungry 121

That book is closed 122

The double evening comes every year 123

Shalom in my mouth like a kumquat, bitter then sweet 124

They were praying 125

A Jew in 2019 126

THERE IS A SEASON

At twilight it began 129

White with sharp talons 130

I lie awake, mid-February 131

Early March thaw 132

Power to the people—or not 134

O frabjous joy, the turkeys 135

How the full moon wakes you 136

At the turning of the tide 137

Praise this tree 138

Gardeners are devout gamblers 139

It's all getting ripe 140

Degradation of the peach 141

Summer, bummer 142

Abundance is wonderful and then it isn't 143

Hottest summer on record 144

A sea change 145

Somehow, communication 146

An argument of crows 147

Visitors at dawn 148

We all live and die here 149

Things to do during a blizzard 151

December 31, night closes in 153

MISHPOCHEH = FAMILY

Hand-me-downs 157

My mother, the Jewish witch 158

Get up and go 160

Her rack of fancy shoes 161

Inside of me as once inside of her 163

Decades have passed 164

Without warning, a door 166

The patrilineal side 167

Casualties 168

Why people include pets in their wills 169

Afternoon of a housecat 170

The rescue kitten 172

Feral no more 173

You're quite gone 175

Sugar Ray slowly leaving 176

Old photo: father 177

My dolls had more clothes than me 178

Early education 179

The karma of heredity 181

Acknowledgments 183

Language Has Shaped My Life

Language has shaped my life

Words are my business. How
I've made house, food, machines
clothing, taxes happen every month.

Words are pointers to fact and lies.
Words are how I shape stories
that map my own and others' lives.

Words go back and forth between us
carrying love and promises, anger
and memories we cherish offkey.

Words jumble themselves into rich
nonsense as I sleep. Are vows
sacred or just shaped air?

When I lie down the final time
will I speak last words or just shut
up, letting silence have its way?

Legacy of a vacant lot

Only us kids used the local vacant lot
mostly the boys and me. We played
cowboys and Indians, we played
war and made a foxhole to duck into.

We all had toy guns, cap pistols
I had a wooden rifle my brother left.
I made up stories we acted out.
My brother was a marine, but often

I wanted to be a guerrilla fighter
appealing to me even at seven.
With a couple of girls who didn't
mind my being a Jew, we were

mamas to our dolls. We married
our cats. We danced hollyhocks
in basins of water. But my heart
belonged to the rough games

in the vacant lot overgrown with
ragweed and bright blue chicory.
That patch of something unbuilt
untamed rooted in me and grew.

The bike gave me wings

I haven't been on a bike in decades
but when I was given my first, age
eleven, it was a passport to even
more freedom than my legs gave me.

Swiftly I pedaled, watching for cars
and their opening doors that knocked
Sandra to the ground, her leg broken.
I flew like a gull [always gulls

from the river passing quickly
overhead through the factories'
belched acid smoke] into the next
neighborhood and the next and next.

I felt like a superhero, freed from ground
to gobble the distance and explore
streets of neat brick houses, big
with attached garages—no factories,

no tool and die shops, no foundries,
no tracks, no smoky bars where men
slumped on stools spending unemployment
checks. Luck sat on the handlebars,

urging faster, farther, never go back.
But as the sun sunk into the elms
I had to return to narrow walls,
loud voices—the doom of family.

The air smelled dirty

Everyone burned coal in our neighborhood,
soft coal they called it from the mountains
of western Pennsylvania where my father
grew up and fled as soon as he could, where
my Welsh cousins dug it down in the dark.

The furnace it fed stood in the dank
basement, its many arms upraised
like Godzilla or some other monster.
It was my job to pull out clinkers
and carry them to the alley bin.

Mornings were chilly, frost on windows
etching magic landscapes. I liked
to stand over the hot air registers
the warmth blowing up my skirts.
But the basement scared me at night.

The fire glowed like a red eye through
the furnace door and the clinkers fell
loud and the shadows came at me as
mice scampered. The washing machine
was tame but the furnace was always hungry.

Ambitious at fourteen

A door-to-door salesman sold the *Encyclopaedia
Britannica* to my mother. My father would
never have spent such money for books.
Bought on installment, of course they

paid far too much. At fourteen,
I decided I would read through, thus
absorbing all knowledge. Before I won
a scholarship and went off to Ann Arbor

I got partway through C. Thus I knew
about aardvarks, anacondas and atlases,
about bees, Bedouins and Berkeley
[the philosopher; the city would come

much later], Canada and caucuses
but never got to Cincinnati or coral.
I assume they put it in a garage
sale before decamping for Florida

as they were moving into a trailer
with no room for aardvarks, atlases or
Zorastrians. Now it's completely online
but has shed that glamour of black

volumes with gold printing that seemed
to my naïve eyes the ultimate knowing, far
more impressive than PhDs or quiz show
winners, and I was going to gobble it all.

Late to find me

In my adolescence, high school
and through college, I was amorphous.
I had not located my boundaries
or built them. If someone looked

into my eyes for long, I fell in love.
I cried at any sad story. Every time
I was moved by a novel or film,
I became one of the characters.

My body was a changing room
where I tried on heroines, villains,
victims. I was Romeo and then
Mercutio, but never Juliet. I knew

even then balconies were not my
forte. Every month a new role
to overplay. Mirrors told me nothing
useful. Lovers gave me scripts

I threw away soon enough. Then
I married a French physicist: between
those steel walls of tradition, I banged
my head and ouch I knew myself.

Images in oil

In San Francisco I worked
as an artist's model. I'd
done so briefly in college,
the easiest job I'd ever

endured. Just sitting
trying not to move. Maybe
a bit chilly but far better
than false smiling my way

through secretarial
boredom, talking poor
women into buying dresses
they couldn't afford,

working the longdistance
switchboard while cock-
roaches pranced and I
hoisted my hand begging

to be allowed to pee.
It was the era of figurative
SF oils. My figure among
others. I got on with artists

and their wives who under-
stood I had no interest

in bedding their husbands.
All I wanted was to get paid

put on my clothes and go
home. Sometimes the artist's
vision of me embodied soft
fantasy or stark nightmare.

At home I'd stare long
in the mirror, wondering
if the reflection I saw
was truth or my delusion

Save me

At the MSPCA dogs were barking
in terror and anger; older cats
looked at us in hopeless appeal
from their cages. In the cage
of kittens, one black and beige

girl reached out through bars
and grabbed Woody's arm. Take
me, take me, Xena cried. Picked
up she purred madly. Purred
in the car all the way home.

I was a poor Jewish girl from
the black ghetto, mad to escape
family, the neighborhood, Detroit,
friends pregnant at sixteen, gang
raped at thirteen, whore at twelve.

Xena could smell death. I didn't
know the university was great but it
was miles away. An alumni group
visited our school interviewing
scholarship applicants. I assumed

a girly persona I hoped would
save me, smiled not too much.
I invented hobbies, mentioned

tutoring and tennis, playing piano
[that was true]. Yes, I had friends

at school [other outcasts], in my
neighborhood; yes, I dated when
studies permitted [I had lovers
in eighth and ninth grades but
had never gone on an actual date];

I had a steady boyfriend for a year,
yes, but he got too serious. I made
the scholarship. At college, all A's
but back to my radical loudmouth
sexually busy Jewish self.

Xena is huge, a hunter; treats
the other cats as kittens. She's
never more than a foot away
day or night from us, taking care.
We both saved our young lives.

Argos, decades ago

for Anastasia with whom I spoke Greek after too long

I remember the magpies natty
in black and white under the gnarled
twisty trunks and matte grey leaves
of old olive trees.

Fallen olives lay in the grass
beneath like the shiny black backs
of beetles. The peasant woman
who gave us water cold

from her well said the magpies
steal. She said the same thing
of the gypsies camped in the valley
below. In those days

they traveled with gaudy big
wheeled carts pulled by thin horses.
They were passing through too, but
a camera did our stealing.

We climbed a dusty path among
sharp grey rocks past dung beetles
pushing their balls up the slope.
At the top a cloud rolled in

and smothered the view. We could
hear rain falling below us but sun
burned our shoulders, our heads.
We ate bread and mizithra

still crosshatched from the netted
bag it hung in. A curious goat came
to watch, then three, then seven
in a circle around us.

I gave them leftover bread. I felt clear
as the sea below on that mountain,
my head empty of fuss: just a calm
body uncoiling in the sun.

The afterlife of old desires

The things we wanted but never got,
those desires that were starved,
stunted, thrust into a dark closet—
what happened to them?

Did they die tragically in their tombs,
like Aida in the last act singing
arias of loss? Or just age like old
letters that yellow and flake to dust?

Are they living in the walls of our
present like mice scuttling at night
to search for crumbs of regret
or hope too slight to maintain them?

Do they imagine returning sonorous
and full throated to claim us again
to pursue those we desired now grey
as lichen and dry as sandpaper?

Do they dream of sprouting one dawn,
mushrooms from vast underground
mycelium? But we've gone on and
they're ghosts no one heeds or fears.

At least a hill

A few people go through life sparsely.
Sometimes it's poverty. I remember
years when what I owned would fit
into one large box, mostly books.

Homeless people push what they can.
For fewer still, it's choice. I taught
poetry once to a traveler who
wandered with backpack and cat.

But most are like me, packing
our apartments, houses with more
than we can ever use. I try to cull,
sending books to library sales

clothes to Goodwill or the thrift
shop, going through drawers full
of kitchen gadgets of dubious use.
Still all I seem to lack is empty

space. Objets d'art of countries
visited, paintings from when I worked
as an artist's model or from friends,
gifts, bargains, mementos, junk.

Neolithic chieftains were buried with
weapons, jewelry, slaves, horses,
chariots. If I were buried with all
my stuff, a mountain would rise.

Night's siren call

Night knocks on the window
Let me in, a voice of moonlight
and wind soughing through trees
that rustle their hunger for rain.

Night calls the young out to dance,
to rut in the bushes and cars
and cheap motels. Thrown cans
and bottles empty along the road

leading backward to meetings.
But in the woods, no neon hook-
ups. Only the foxes dance, white
tails flashing. The raccoons

are busy picking locks. The coy
wolves dream with their teeth.
The owl flies silent as snow
reading the small ones' scuttle.

I stand at the window and imagine
racing through darkness on mouse feet.

The depth waits

That instant between waking
and sleep, I seek and it always
evades me. Unknowable,
ungraspable. Quicksilver.

A door opens suddenly. I
fall through into a volcanic
firestorm of the dying; into
a calm green lake of tears.

Into the room where I slept
thirty years ago, everything
in its place except a mirror
that doesn't reflect my face.

Sleep is a mysterious pool
of uncertain depth. In childhood
my mother was fascinated
by a pond called The Blue Hole

said to be bottomless. A wise-
cracking child I said it can't
go through to China. But sleep's
quite deep enough to drown us.

After the knee is replaced

Pain insulates. Obligations, news
politics fade to a distant traffic
murmur I barely notice and ignore.

Pain isolates: It's so much work
to communicate. Words are heavy
on my tongue as rough bricks.

I lie in a thick-walled fortress
of pain obsessed with pills, exer-
cises that torture my cyborg knee.

I'm useless as a pet store gold
fish imprisoned in a small bowl: back
& forth, forth & back, then sleep.

Post op is essentially a dull hiatus
between my past and the life I want.
I'm a lump that complains too much.

Late fall, temperature 45

Around the town pier I walk
on my new and still painful knees.
The air is crisp as sheets clean
from the line. I can see needles
on pines across the harbor.

One man is motoring his boat
around the pier to be pulled
from the water and stored for cold
weather, storms that will toss
hard waves against the pilings.

Two men who quarrel like lovers
are trying to lower the mast
on their boat *The Guilty Pleasure*.
When I make my slow way around
again they are still at it. The mast

stands straight up like a fuck-you
finger. Two women my age walk
matching dogs. The water rushes
in from the bay but swirls at pier's
end because the sweep of the north

wind is pushing water from the inner
harbor straight out. Which will win?
The air is harsh and strong as neat
whiskey in my lungs. I am alive
still to thrust myself into winter.

Doors opening, closing on us

Maybe there is more of the magical
in the idea of a door than in the door
itself. It's always a matter of going
through into something else. But

while some doors lead to cathedrals
arching up overhead like stormy skies
and some to sumptuous auditoriums
and some to caves of nuclear monsters

most just yield a bathroom or a closet.
Still, the image of a door is liminal,
passing from one place into another,
one state to the other, boundaries

and promises and threats. Inside
to outside, light into dark, dark into
light, cold into warm, known into
strange, safe into terror, wind

into stillness, silence into noise
or music. We slice our life into
segments by rituals, each a door
to a presumed new phase. We see

ourselves progressing from room
to room perhaps dragging our toys
along until the last door opens
and we pass at last into was.

Learning to be quiet

To need to stay busy
is to miss the scent of balsam
on the morning air. To miss
the small sound of a thrasher
kicking up leaves beneath bushes.

So many of the minor pleasures
come to us when we spread
silence around us like a silken
mirror and allow ourselves
to subside into stillness and wait.

Every moment does not need
to be stuffed. Silence is a fullness
not a vacuum. One advantage
of age is to be able to learn
the secrets of an empty room.

Is it empty? Light furnishes it.
The walls, the floor give little
intimate noises as they enclose.
The windows are supplied with trees
tall sky and a crossing crow.

Caught in an electronic spider
web that connects countries, eras,
people we befriend whom we will

never meet, time carries us forward
over rocks in a white splashing whir.

Cats know all about stillness.
When they want to leap, they bend
gravity. When they want to rest
they settle into receptivity,
paws folded like Buddhas.

Doing nothing is not empty. It's
receiving, it's opening, it's
a turning within and a turning
beyond at once. Let the tide
of silence close over your head.

Into the Twilight Zone

Being old at the end of the world

It isn't that I think life will end.
Gaia is ingenious and life breeds
life in new forms. The gorgeous
predators will have succumbed

to the most savage predator
of all. We will have killed off
frogs, half the birds, most fish
whales and bears and butterflies

but something will rise to replace.
We sneer at dinosaurs but they
destroyed little and endured long.
Greed was only born with us.

We didn't invent war. Rats
and ants, chimps and others
fight each other, but with teeth,
claws, superior numbers. But

our wars kill everything around
and damage lasts decades or close

to forever. Gaia will be glad to be
rid of us, her obnoxious tenants.

Our dirt and waste will long out-
last us. Perhaps new lifeforms
will evolve to eat plastic and drink
radiation. They'll have to.

Even wine turns at last to vinegar

My mother gave up gardening
after my father uprooted her from
her network of women friends
to Florida where even air sweats.

I can't grow lettuce or beans, she
said. Not even parsley. I don't
know these plants, they're leathery.
They don't feel green to me.

She collected articles on stroke
but said nothing. She hid her fear
like the dollars stolen from grocery
money doled out to her weekly.

A local artist and gardener who could
no longer tend her beds said *Look
how beautiful are the weeds and see
how the daylilies live with them.*

Some things we cannot accept
as our bodies lose themselves
one organ at a time. Some things
we can. Vinegar is good for salads.

A reckoning in flesh

My good body, the horse
I've ridden through high roiling water
and wind scoured desert, over
barely marked trails of broken stone:
there is no horse. I am the horse.

You are slower now. I am slower.
I have seams where implements
have been inserted. I no longer
dance all night, dance partners
down. Walk miles all day for pleasure.

I am my own fate. Inside is my death.
What storm will tear my entrails?
My faithful clock of a heart
will run down. The skull longs
to shine in moonlight, bare at last.

Anne Boleyn knew the hour of her end
yet hoped till the last second Henry
would relent. But most of us think
of death only in the well of night
while fiery stars wheel over our beds.

Space is the coldest cold. But I live
on a smaller scale where ice threatens
and two degrees make a fever. Body,
you are just me and I'm just you
no matter how I punish and reward.

She is letting go now

She is leaving her red shiny shoes.
She is leaving her Burberry
trench coat bought two decades
ago in London with the lover
she thought was her last.

She has abandoned her books
carted from coast to coast
and back again, with their corners
of pages turned down, her snark
in the margins, her question marks.

She is leaving her most recent
lover although mostly they went
to movies together and had supper
although sometimes he took
Viagra. She too is often weary.

She is leaving her medicine
cabinet with the rows of pills

that were supposed to save her.
She is not leaving her brass bed
although very soon she will.

She is leaving her computer, full
of work and emails from friends
unanswered, but mostly she worries
about the faithful cat who purrs
against her, unaware she is leaving.

Leftovers

A jigsaw puzzle of the Grand Canyon
with pieces missing. It has been on her
table at least a year, maybe a decade
Was she expecting the pieces to return

to her? A fine layer of dust lies on it.
The table itself clean—enough to eat
on she'd have said. She liked sayings.
They were easy on the tongue.

In the trash, cans of Campbell soup,
chicken noodle, turkey noodle, mushroom,
asparagus. Did she live on soup toward
the end? A beige cardigan folded

over a chair back. Bunny slippers
wait beside the carefully made bed.
A note to herself: pay electric bill,
clean aquarium. Her son who lives

in Arizona gave her tropical fish. "I
don't know why," she said, "I can't pet
them, they don't know me. He hasn't
been back since." Many photographs

in silver-plated frames—herself younger,
the two husbands, both on the mantel

now, her live son and the dead one
in uniform. Who will want them now?

We are there and then we aren't,
our detritus left behind for Good Will
and the dump, unless some still living
friend needs a souvenir or two.

I knew a woman who worked for a bank.
When someone with a trust there died
she'd clean out their home. "Isn't it sad?"
I asked. She looked at me. "It's just a job."

What goes faster every time I turn around

How odd that as I age
I move slower
and time runs twice as fast.

When I was little, school
took three years to pass,
ring upon ring of hours.

When I was young, summer
vacation was as long
as seabirds can fly.

High school classes froze
my brain and sawdust words
took eons to filter down.

In my twenties, a month
long love affair could hurt
to vanishing like train tracks.

Death belonged to other
people. Every promise was
forever and several days.

Now time runs through
the sieve of my veined hands
and is gone, is gone, is gone.

Ultimate ultimatum

The body whines in the afternoon,
you overdid me. Lay me down now.
You think I'm made of steel?
Why didn't you stop when I begged?

The body rants in the night, waking
the mind. I told you so! I'm angry
and you'll know it. See if I let you sleep.
You have no idea how many sore

muscles I can light up, places
in me you never noticed before.
Who expects a little finger
to scream like a tiger in rage?

You think you're having a heart
attack? You should be so lucky.
Your stomach is volcanic. Bet
you can't find your spleen—yet.

You've taken me for granted far
too many decades. Now, my turn
to grab your undivided attention.
It's all me now till the very end.

For your information—from
your pharmacist

Do not take this medicine with dairy products.
Do not take this medicine with any medication
containing aluminum, calcium, bismuth, iron or zinc.
Do not take this product with vitamins or minerals.

This medicine may cause dry mouth or arrhythmia.
This medicine may cause diarrhea, nausea,
vomiting, hair loss, dizziness, sore joints.
This medicine may cause insomnia.

Discontinue this medicine if you black
out frequently, if your heart stops
or if you cannot breathe for half
an hour. Discontinue if death ensues.

Otherwise take four a day.
Continue until medication is completely
consumed, or you are.

It diminishes

As we age, the circles around us
shrink. The generation before us
who ran the town, had us to dinner,
told us stories of before we moved

here, have almost all gone into earth
or air. Now half of our own pack
have vanished. Too many memorials,
too often the ambulance wails.

How far I can walk or hobble goes
from six miles to down the hill
to the road and back. Hi there
I hurt chirps a new joint or muscle.

What can I see or hear now?
What can I lift, carry, how deep
can I dig? What do I daily forget?
I batter on these closing-in walls.

Do we now chat with doctors instead
of colleagues? Texts, Facebook aren't
having coffee together, sharing
days that are no longer so full.

The longest lesson

Our cats and dogs teach us about
dying as they have shown us
our own aging, again and again
with each new life that sinks
to its end, a furry mirror.

I grew up before death was erased
from everyday life. People often
died at home and we watched
their passing, we held their hands
and saw death creep over them, then

we shut their eyes—because
we can't endure that blank
gelid gaze with the light turned
off. But still I never quite
expected I'd age like others.

Somehow I'd be immune, running
up stairs and dancing all night.
Surprise! I'm just another mammal
with a pain here and another there
and that door at the end of the hall.

Praise in spite of all

I thank the cool night that let me sleep.
I thank the bright morning that wakes me.
I thank the birds who peep and carol
celebrating the return of daylight.

I do not thank the spiny black gypsy
moths eating my trees to death.
Who rain shit all sticky on my roof
I thought at first were drops of rain.

I thank my cats for their warm bodies
against my own, for their healing purr,
for their companionship in all weathers
of pain, of loss, of loneliness.

I do not thank the ticks who climb
my leg bearing a smorgasboard
of diseases of which I've already
had two, draculas drinking my blood.

I thank cookbooks out of whose stained
pages fine meals are born. I thank
poetry that speaks right into me, music
moving through me, tales that engulf.

I do not praise greedy idiots who poison
the sea, the air, food, bees and us. I do

not praise those who stand on the bodies
of those they consider less human.

I thank my long love who has endured
these decades with me, the house
and life we have built brick by bloody
brick and still together inhabit.

I thank what I can as I age toward
the end. So much is beautiful, friends
are kind, I have loved many and
some even have loved me. Amein.

Taking stock in fall

The first yellow, orange, red leaves
eddy down to the wet bricks.
Reluctantly but in its season
the maple lets go of its clothes.

I too am letting go, not willingly
but of necessity. Long walks
in the woods, by the sea I
can no longer manage. Swims

forbidden in the sandy ponds.
I'll never climb another peak.
Flying has become arduous.
Dancing is a memory but still

I cook, I raise veggies, flowers
for food and pleasure. We take
short trips, I play with, care for
my cats. We make love, we

listen to music, I read a book
a week, write two poems, eat
with friends, observe Shabbat:
a long life still full of joy.

A good death?

What is a good death? One you
anticipate so you can plan it,
make necessary arrangements.

A sudden death so there's little
suffering, not months of hospital.
Just bang and you're out of it.

Dying in your sleep with no
pain, just went to bed and never
got up. Hard on who finds you.

Suicide? It's chosen, you're
in charge but careful where
you do it. And don't botch it.

Death is something that loved
ones or those responsible are
left to clean up, make sense of.

As lost friends touch my mind
I worry about those I love
who'll remain, deal, are dealt with.

The sum of mortality

When I am dead:
I'll never do another load of laundry
never have to cook a fancy meal when I'm tired
never have to watch another friend or cat age and die
never have to see another doctor, take another pill
never see the inside of a hospital again, patient or visitor
never again have to deal with power or cable company
never squirm through another sleepless night
never have to watch politicians destroy and corrupt
never have to deal with critics who hate me
never watch us slide into another war
never endure my sore back or neck or weak eyes
never again diet or try to
never be haunted by words I should have swallowed
by what I did or should have done and didn't.

When I am dead:
I will never lie flesh to flesh with the one I love
never smell a rose with damask or gallica in its genes
or pick lilacs or bury my face in a peony I've grown
never plunge my hands into rich soil to plant
never be purred to sleep with a soft paw on my shoulder
never see the fields of daffodils whose bulbs we buried
never walk in the woods on old sand roads
never come over the dune and see the ocean roaring below

never again read a novel that pulls me into its world
never again eat, drink and gossip evenings away with friends
never feel sun on my face and back or watch birds at the feeders
never sit with a happy cat in my lap gazing into my eyes
never see my beloved's face again
never write another poem.

A profitable undeath

In previous times, people said
you went to the hospital to die. Now
near the end you are kept a zombie
helplessly undead against your will.

Tubes stuck here and there
penetrate your soft issues
and every tender orifice.
Machines breathe and digest.

All the while the bills grow
like tumors. Doctors forbid you
to give your body back so you
can finally, finally let go.

It still makes us happy

There's a comfort in old bodies
coming together—far more gently
these days, more like peonies
opening than bear cubs wrestling.

You know so well what excites,
what pleases, what works for the other
that body almost as familiar
as your own arms and face.

You trust absolutely. You know
how to lead or follow. If we
don't break the bed any longer
we find huge comfort therein.

War of the old

Mondays I'd call her.
Father would go to play
bridge at the community center
and she'd be home alone.

"I used to think it was sad
to be alone," she said.
I could tell she was cupping
the phone, her voice soft

to keep him from hearing
eight blocks away. "He"—
a word always italicized—
"he sits there on the couch

supervising me as if I
haven't been cleaning
house eighty years." Oh
Mother I see old couples

in the supermarket aisle
fighting over which crackers
to buy. Husbands who have
no one left to boss around

except their wives, wives
for whom complaining
is comfortable as soup.
Aging opens all the cracks.

Who can hold them, what can save them?

When my mother died, when my grandmother
died, all those memories I never got to catch
and keep vanished to dust motes floating
in a skein of silver moonlight and gone.

Maybe I am a poet in part because I want
to seize all those memories that flit
and vanish and seal them into the perfect
resinous jewels of amber, moments transfixed

and perfected like Jurassic wasps. Questions
I never thought to ask in childhood hang
like dead birds around my neck. Never will
I know my great-grandfather the rabbi's

first name or what his wife was like. How
did Grandma Hannah get along with her
mother? Was that who told her all those
tales of golems and dybbuks she passed

on to me, more precious than the dolls'
clothes she sewed from scraps of old
dresses? They both told stories but
never enough, parts of their lives edited

out, too caked with old blood, too harsh
in the mouth like lye. Even though I write
forty or fifty books, my private memories
will ride the wind away like milkweed fluff.

Joy to the world

Now I must learn to understand, to accept
deaths of those I've loved, the pain
of weak joints, memory full of holes
that days, faces slip through.

There is no other life but this with all
its grime and guts. Breathing becomes an art.
Every morning is still new and the sun rises
whether we see it or not.

Every flower is a gift I've lived to smell.
Love glows more intensely in the twilight.
I polish old memories, amber taking on
heat and power till they shine.

There is no boredom now for each moment
is precious as a kitten and requires much
care. What can I take for granted now?
My own hand is strange to me.

I dream less and sleep more deeply.
I let ambition rise, drift off like a helium
filled balloon until it's just a speck,
free of its prods and jerks.

I sit in every hour seeking to enjoy it.
Everything slow ebbs and glides

away, away. My body has it own agenda
carrying me along.

Praise my aching body that still gives
me pleasure in the arms of my long love.
Praise the land that feeds me and many wild
creatures, that still gives

me joy in each season with its colors
and otherness. Praise friends who help
and companion me. Praise my cats
with their loyalty.

So much of my life was struggle
to survive, to learn, to write what
I had to, to find love. I let go of all
but love now till the end.

U.S.

Dirge for my country

My country, you are hurtling us into a dark
morass. In that old war, I understood
the Vietcong better than I understood
the Pentagon. Alienated, at daily war
in the streets and movement lofts
against my government, yet I felt hope at least
sometimes that we were pushing hard
enough to birth a dream of equality.

Step by step those with stifled voices
those dealt day by day fresh wounds
in their minds, their backs, their cunts
their very skin punished for itself
moved a step closer to evident selfhood,
a step closer to that picnic
in the sun of dignity on the grass
of survival, our cultures melding.

We seemed to be growing up slowly
to a willingness to listen to those
who don't look like our mirror image,
to those we perhaps had feared
and turned to bogeyman shadows.
We seemed to be almost arriving

at something halfway holy and adult.
Was it all seeming? All a moment?

We are rushing backward to a war
against our best selves. We're suckling
hatred, eating hatred for breakfast
and lunch, snacking on hatred, fattening
on it, bloated with it. We'll dance on
corpses of good ideas. We'll burn
dissenters like witches. Is this the end
of good my country might've done?

Way late December 2016

A cold rain pushes in on the wind
dashing sideways into my eyes
and hair. A lone gull is blown
almost inside out like an umbrella

his wings outspread. He dives
to a roof and settles, still ruffled
and spiky. The bare trees bend.
The oaks' tough leaves tear loose.

It's close enough to the shortest
day that it never feels quite light.
This is the butt end of the year.
It's hard to celebrate what's coming:

hard times for those of us not rich.
Times when the overlords gloat
and I search for something good
like a pig rooting in sour mud.

The news of the day is grey and dark;
it explodes shards into my ears,
my eyes. Danger rides the wind
like ash and chokes me as I breathe.

Consider these but you won't

Consider the child with curly brown
hair sleeping with her dog in the back
of an old SUV while her parents doze
in scruffy front seats tilted back.

Consider the child with brown skin
called the "N" word and told to go back
to Africa, whose great-grandparent
built the road running past the school.

Consider the woman pregnant from
rape, the woman who could not take
off work to cross two states for
an abortion, who tries hard to love

her child but he looks more and
more like that nightmare rapist.
Consider men and women who worked
the assembly line till their ears

dimmed out, back, kidneys rotted
wanting a pension to reward them
with sunshine. But the company
no longer has to pay its promises.

Consider the family whose home
will be taken by the bank while they

can no longer pay for the pills
for cancer that cost a month's wages

every month. So their daughter
dies and they're still in debt. But
Herr President, you cannot even
see them; they're just too small.

Tyr marches on

What a mishmash our weeks
suggest: okay, sun and moon.
Odin, Thor: a bow to Nordic
ancestors. Somehow a Roman
god snuck in on Shabbat.

Tuesday sticks out among
the motley bunch. I must've
looked it up a dozen times
or more. Who ever heard
of Tyr? Forgotten god of war.

I wish we could forget war
but since I was a toddler,
we've always been fighting
usually for some hyped up
excuse or whipped up scam.

Mars, Ares, those are the gods
that in reality we worship what-
ever pallid rituals we go through
in places marked for prayer. Tyr
is still top god. Hail Tuesday!

U.S.

We force children to go to school
Schools are shooting galleries
We force children to experience death

Don't go to a concert
                    you might die
Don't go to the mall
                    you might die
Don't go to pray
                    you might die
Don't go to the movies
                    you might die
Above all, don't go to college
                    you might die

Every bullet sprayed is money
for some corporation
Every child who dies
is profit for the NRA
Every murder brings contributions
to senators, congressmen, governors
and a President who couldn't care less

How much do we care
if the child bleeding out
is not ours
We live in a gun-happy country.
Some grow richer
Some never come home
Some never grow up

Their mouths are closed

They are dying all over the world
those tongues that defined a people,
the mother's voice that first gave
names to what they saw and felt.

The last words in those languages
rise in ghost mist from dying
mouths and a whole world
evaporates and never was.

Each word gave light and meaning,
marking what was important,
what dangerous, what holy. No
one will say that name again.

Into soil goes the body of the last
speaker and silence grows like grass.

Can't you hear them?

Listen carefully every morning,
afternoon, night, hear the crying
of children yanked from mothers

torn from fathers by brutal
strangers, without explanation
without pity, without mercy—

locked away in crowded dorms
with predators and other kids
who know no more than they do.

My French husband was taken
from his parents when they fled
the Nazis into Switzerland.

He was scarred for life, always
convinced his parents loved
his younger brother more.

Kids think their parents could
have kept them, wonder what
they did wrong to be locked up.

Will they ever again see their mothers?
The government judges them so trivial

why bother with accurate records?

I hear them crying like hungry
birds, I hear their terror and pain
like distant thunder rumbling.

In cages, they huddle. Such pain
won't dissipate but sinks into
our names and brains, our history.

Illegal with only hope

The mother imagines [a few more
steps, another push across a mine
field, just one more night hiding
in rank bushes] she can carry

her child across the border
to some kind of safety, anything
better than what she flees, hauling
her child through the fields of hell.

She has a wound on her leg
untended, unbandaged, bleeding
now and then when weeds, branches
brush it. She has a deep wound

inside: the wan face of her older child
as the life drained from it with
blood from the blast that tore
his flesh apart. The dusty body

of her husband fallen into a ditch,
the ditch where she huddled holding
tight the still living child who is all
she can imagine of any future.

So she slogs forward toward
that invisible border where mothers
can keep their children safe,
perhaps, in a world on fire.

Ladies who judge

They're very charitable
they tell you, sitting on boards
that dole out money [never
enough] to those who need it.

They are very concerned
with who is worthy, who
deserves, as if every empty
stomach, human, dog, cat

or bird doesn't need filling.
There is a certain way
they speak of those who
have less than they enjoy.

A certain expression in eyes,
an attitude of sugared lye:
I slump across a conference
table squashing down anger,

my desire to push them off
their high comfortable chairs.
I want them to sleep in door-
ways, on the street tonight,

to sift through Goodwill piles
seeking a shabby warm coat

that almost fits, to live as I did
on water and flour, three weeks

of oatmeal, two of smelt. You
think your bank account makes
you worthy to judge, to give
or deny. But I judge you now:

guilty of unearned superiority,
guilty of spiteful condescension,
of believing those you should be
serving are less entitled than you.

Joiners

The creek burbles along, grows
wider, deeper, meanders,
becomes a tributary to a river.

It flings itself into the moving
water, joins the currents, part
now of what is bigger, stronger.

A person joins a group, a party,
a team, a mob. A person becomes
one with the others, absorbed,

sharing with others now kin
the intent, the goal, rhetoric,
idioms, us versus them outside.

We all long at times to be swallowed
absorbed into a fast-moving river
carried along in its strength.

We may not guess where it's bound
or we may not really care, just so
we belong and others know it.

I can't write a love poem

To write about love
in this volcanic time
when shards of hatred
litter the streets, when murder

feels like a parlor game.
But if we can't feel for
each other, how can we
care about a child caged

or a mother drowned
as an overloaded boat
sinks in sight of a shore
of refuge, a girl raped

into submission, a boy
handed a rifle at ten, cats
gassed in shelters, calves
penned from their mothers

crying for her milk. How
can we feel anything but
raw urges if we can't love
a partly broken dear one?

We are all half unmade
full of preprogrammed
desires for mannequins
and cars that can't love us.

We have only each botched
other to help us through
the mud that wants to drown
us, close up our eyes, shut

our mouths so we can't speak
clumsy truths aloud to men
fat and shiny with power they'll
burn the world down to keep.

Noon in a three-star restaurant

He eats a good lunch, the senator
who hates women, especially
those who don't smile enough
don't polish his ego or prick.
Pain is good for their souls.

He has a classic dry martini,
the senator who votes to strip
food stamps from children,
health care from old ladies,
clean water from everyone.

He enjoys a hearts of palm salad
while a stream runs through his brain,
white, pure as new ice. He knows
who his real friends are, donors.
People with darker skin: can't

you see how dirty they are? A Kobe
steak, death by chocolate. Money
from oil, big pharma, insurance,
utilities, the extremely rich. We're
superfluous. Nothing to offer

except our lives, our health,
taxes, bodies for endless wars.
He does not represent us
although he spouts the right
clichés that light up brains.

The President speaks

"You can always go to another
state" to have your abortion
just so long as you're rich,
have a nanny to watch your

kids, can take off from your
job, have a ride available
or your own car, aren't
living at home or needing

to hide the procedure. Yes
affluent women could fly
to Puerto Rico while the rest
of us were doing it to ourselves,

dying of back-alley butchery,
bleeding to death, left sterile
from botched operations,
yes, we can always just die,

Mr. Trump, and many mothers
will be leaving their children
to be raised by others, many
teenagers will drop out of school,

many women will die alone
in their bloody beds. It will
be just the way you like it
for women who dare to choose.

This is our legacy

How will they curse us,
the 3rd, 4th generations,
the ones that survive
the deaths we left them.

How could we explain
the world on fire, species
wiped out daily, oceans
with more plastic than fish?

That we let a corrupt man
stomp refugees fleeing
rape, murder and hunger
that we let him set blazes

no one could put out.
We saw the cliff ahead
We were well warned
We took everyone over.

That was how our world
ends, in lies and greed
vast and numerous maggots
dining on the corpse of hope.

Endless rage

I have needed my anger often
enough. It saved me from rape,
gave me that red roar of energy
that sent me out of bad beds.
Let me shed insults like a dog
shaking off drops of rain.

But anger can poison with a slow
leak into the blood. Anger
can turn on the nearest, the weak,
the ones who can't retaliate.
Fume against anyone you wouldn't
choose to have as neighbors.

The unlike, those who have less
and thus must be less and should
be and have less and occupy less
space and live less. Those who
love differently and likely more,
who have a different god or color.

We are a dangerous people
who plunge into war after war,
who hand out automatic weapons
like tax rebates, who express shock
when angry men do exactly what
they want and kill and kill and kill.

The rain comes on like a tide

Maples and oaks are tossing
their green tresses as rain plays
kettledrums on every roof.

The sky is low as the ceiling
of a tunnel and almost as dark.
Petals litter the ground

from peonies, rhododendrons.
Step out, sink in. You're soaked
in five minutes. Wind shoves

grit into your eyes. The earth
feels angry and why not?
She's sick of our poisons.

More wildfires, daily tornadoes
stronger hurricanes, nor'
easters that tear at the coast:

we've attacked our mother
for centuries. Why shouldn't
the weather fight us back?

Another request comes in

The cruelty in any given day
rises like an acid tsunami.
A man rapes a woman because
he can. An army invades, killing
whole families, whole villages
burnt because they can.

A woman tells her son how
ugly he is, because she can.
There's no one else to hear.
Her malice is safe, bruises
hidden under clothes, invisible.
He kicks his dog afterward.

A rich man blocks health care
for those who have less than
he does. A woman bleeds
to death and her daughter
finds her, because legislators
think women who have sex

deserve all the pain they can
inflict. A mother holds her dying
child whose belly is swollen,

eyes jelly, though she gave
her last crumb to him, just
another casual casualty.

We have seen all this on TV,
we have heard it all before.
It's not my fault, we mutter.
Only a short way to not my
business, not my concern.
They're always asking for money.

Charleston massacre

He had grown bloated
on the red hot empty calories
of rightwing race hatred.

He carried his gun hidden
in his pants like sex power
into a church to murder.

What safer place to slaughter?
On city streets someone else
might be carrying, but church

was guaranteed to let him
kill without danger to himself.
Black, brown, caramel faces

praying. Easy for him as paper
targets at a shooting range, like
mechanical ducks crossing

on a midway. How brave I am
he thought as he shot them down
preacher, mother, teacher, other

to him whose white skin's a license:
the right to hate, the right to seek
the defenseless and gorge on blood.

Call to action

It's only a short life
between a pale dawn
and a garish sunset.

It's only a short life:
why not use it? What
we ignore comes back

to bite us in the ass.
What we fail to do
rots, breeding maggots.

We are covered in lies
so it's hard to see,
hard to breathe deeply.

We say, why were we
chosen to struggle when
the task is rock heavy?

Turn the TV to a cartoon;
go out for fast food.
Bar the door. Sleep tight.

The assaults in the street

aren't aimed at you yet.
Why bother to be bothered?

We were born in bad times
when murder is patriotic,
hatred, a golden banner.

What can we do? Some-
thing's more than nothing.
Pick up a rock, ax, a mike,

your cell, a painted sign.
It's only a short life.
Spend it well.

Love Is No Accident

⋮

Am I pretty enough?

In spring after mating turkey hens
go off to lay eggs and brood alone.
Yesterday I saw three males displaying
their tail fans to each other, useless.

I could see in gobblers silly male vanity
but I remember flirting, primping
displaying vainly before some
boy or man I found attractive.

So much effort for women, right
clothes, hair done, nails, wax. Did you
have to diet, starve? Now you put
yourself out like a tray of warm cookies.

So it goes when we need to couple.
Sex makes idiots of us all.

Much too early marriage

I put on my first marriage
like a girdle my skinny body
didn't need. Within compression
I sweated blood and it hurt.

When I finally tore it off I
confused a man who believed
women were born wearing
girdles and rocking cradles.

I liked wine; he liked water.
I liked sex; he endured it
as a duty. I loved cats.
He disciplined our stray.

I was all red and orange.
He was a modest grey.
I was garlic and roses;
he, lemon and lawn grass.

Loud rock music versus
a string quartet. Knives
v. spoons. Astonishing we
stayed bound almost two years.

French lessons

I was impressed watching my French
father-in-law peeling an apple
in one long unfurling strand.

He used a knife. I have tried
with a peeler and still the skin
breaks, never a perfect spiral.

I was surprised when my French
husband stubbed his toe, not
shouting ow! but iiiieeeee!

So I learned sounds we think
instinctive, the way we sneeze,
they're all a product of culture.

Listening to Parisian children
shouting in the street below
I felt thoroughly American.

I sometimes dreamed in French
but could never write in it,
language structuring my brain.

I'd thought myself citizen
of the world but found Detroit
had gone into my bones.

Chicago one summer

An apartment on the second floor
corner of 55th, a building leaking
the scent of decay and old dinners,
loud music, jagged angry voices

a dog barking like an endless
cough. It was our second place
after Paris, my French husband
and me and a found black kitten.

We had begun to fray, poor
graduate students living on
offal and rice, a week of smelt
gallon wine, cheapest cat food.

We were all always hungry.
I was hungry for what I'd had
with other men. He disappeared
into the cyclotron for weeks.

When he emerged, I was a pit
he feared to fall into. Silence
was his best weapon. I knew
only his turned back in bed.

I felt myself evaporating.
I was thin, needy and ragged.
I gave off dark red pheromones

like a cat in heat and men came.

I chose one who understood
my poetry was not a hobby.
I used him as an ax to chop
myself free and bled guilt.

Goodbye sad dark apartment,
goodbye cat to a better home
with people who could feed her.
Goodbye marriage that caved in.

The various flavors of argument

Squabbling can be a form of flirtation
or a covert attack disguised as a simple
request or complaint—or just a puff
of annoyance gone like aerosol spray.

Long lovers know the pressure
points, the old scars from childhood
fights and putdowns, love curdled,
all the old relationship bruises

that never really heal, every one.
We drag behind us a heavy train
of our past from the first loud cry
to the most recent betrayal.

It's a job of heavy excavation
even to see each other clearly.
How often we're really fighting
with an ex instead of our partner.

Fighting can act like a summer
thunderstorm leaving all clean
and bright. Or it can tear through
the body like a scythe.

While it dies

The last weeks of a dead
marriage are full of trenches
filled with barbed wire
and rotting promises.

The last weeks of a dead
marriage are to be fought
through like a jungle
of poisonous vines.

You wonder if you can
possibly escape alive.
You wonder if you must
kill him to get out.

Love is something you
doubt, a past the nasty
present has wiped away
with a dirty cloth.

Conversations are fencing
matches with scimitars.
Anger paints the air
till it screams.

This is a chess game
with burning pieces.
This is all you have left
of history and hope.

Remnants of a dead marriage

What are the remains a man
who has gone off tearing a hole
in the wall the rain slants through
may leave behind scattered here

and there through the scavenged
house? A sock under the bed
they shared then occupied part-
time by another he preferred.

Photographs in which lost time
is pinned down like dead butter-
flies that age slowly to flakes
of dust. A ring he gave her,

promises rotting with a stench
of cadaver, a painting that wasn't
even a sketch when abandoned,
stories that lost their endings.

Every so often on a fine May day
a button from a shirt turns up
as she sweeps. She holds it
on her palm, then throws it away.

Fooled again, she said

It's been a hard and scary winter
so far, frozen chickadee on the porch,
wild turkeys mobbing us as they skid
on the ice, demanding food. Parsnips

under mulch frozen solid. Pitch pines
splintered by gale-force winds. Then
comes a January thaw two, three days.
Snow softens to puddles. Icicles drip

to vanishment. We can see bare ground
again. The air feels gentle as a warm
bath. We're let out like kids at recess
to walk our own land again, assessing.

It's false spring. Like in a bad marriage
or a dangerous affair, the partner
is kind suddenly, maybe brings flowers
or a necklace, belts out arias of love.

You think that's how it's going to be
again, like it was at the beginning.
Tomorrow a blizzard. Tomorrow his
fist'll be just as quick and hard.

Time dims it

After so long you might as well
forgive. The anger won't ignite
just faded greyish clinkers. Re-
member? You stifle a yawn.
No heat left, no danger.

Once that anger was a rod
of sun-colored molten steel
replacing bone in your back.
It was the noise kept you
awake all and every night.

It was the light that woke
you every morning scratching
on your lids, your own rooster
crowing in your belly, rise
go out and seek revenge.

Now you can take his hand
soft as it always was,
cool as you might recall
on your thigh, if you're
willing to remember.

You're just subway passengers
avoiding eye contact who
speak different languages.
You almost miss your anger
but the silence caresses you.

Where do pet names go in the end?

All lovers have private languages
that evolve out of fact and fantasy
over time, when there's time enough.

Names that are silly and plush.
Words for parts of the body, certain
acts they enjoy or don't. When

that relationship dies, those words
feel sticky and sad, something sweet
spilled on a counter that glues itself

to your arm, that stains your sleeve.
We want to forget them unless we
still love—in which case they turn salt

and sharp, crystals that gouge valleys
in our flesh like knives, until we
finally forgive the one who left.

The cemetery of spent passions

Of all the husbands and lovers
how many did you really care for?
How many do you ever even
remember with strong emotion?

You regret lost and dead friends
with more honest energy; you
mourn your buried cats and for
them you shed real salt tears.

I remember one of my female
lovers with a mix of regret
and anger; my first male lover
almost killed me. I should

weep for him? The ones—
friends before we fell into bed—
they get little shrines on the hill
of the cemetery of spent passions.

Those I worked with, yes, they
too have stone monuments of honor.
Earlier husbands were mixed bags;
domesticity has its knives, needles

and pillows, but only the best
longest love is notched on my
spine, burned into my brain
will in dying be my last thought.

That wild rush

The alewives throw themselves forward
upstream thrashing, a power so intense
the seagulls stabbing fish right next
to them are ignored. Uphill they hump

the rushing river, over rocks. The force
of mating makes them indifferent
to danger, to fatigue, to death that waits
upstream when they at last succeed.

Sex drove me against stones when I was
young, pushed me into beds of nails
my blood boiling in me, blind to how
stupid, how rigid, how weak or mean

was the object where my need focused.
I wonder how I survived that wild rush
to grow wiser if no less sensual, to
choose finally a mate capable of love.

No regrets

You say, I wish I had known you
at twenty, at twenty-five, at thirty.
No, you don't, I say, you weren't,
I wasn't ready.

The dreams we sweated out in
uncertain nights and strange beds,
we had to suffer through them
to the acid core.

We had stories to trudge through
visions to use up into mist
and drizzle, fantasies to smoke
to dull ash.

We weren't ripe yet, my love.
We needed all those years apart
before we were shaped to come
firmly together.

Every botched loving, every torn
promise, every mistaking a mirror
for a person, they all taught us
how to love at last.

We cannot regret our wanderings
no matter how hard and cold.
They brought us to each other
and home.

Let me never count the ways

There are so many ways of making love:
there is paying the bills on time
every bloody month so we don't owe
interest. There is interest ratcheted up
for the 4th draft, for the thirteenth telling
of the story. There is the tale never told
because it would embarrass.

There is the coffee brewed at six
when your hands are still huge with sleep.
There is the rosemary chicken sautéed
when I am way too tired to stand.
There is the walk shoveled all the way
down to the road. There is the laundry
done every Monday every week every
year. There is the football game
recorded. The phone call blocked.

There is the tenderness that lasts
until the trees turn to leaf mold.
There is the care that surrounds
and laves the sore back and weary
shoulders but lets go for freedom's

sake. There is the love that stands
guard and the love that keeps quiet.

Yes, we make love in bed and on
the couch, but we also make love
out of toast and nails and vacuum
cleaners, out of needles and thread,
out of ink and kitty litter, out of hours
and days given to each other not
because we must but from desire.

Fire in winter

Outside winter slams against
the windows, ice crystals
pricking whoever dares go out.

The wind pulls at the cedar
shingles, pushes at the roof,
tears branches loose and sends

them as missiles through grey
air. But inside it's summer
we're making, a radiant June

day in our bed. Your chest
almost scalds me with sun
and your arms are balmy.

We make our own season: with
the friction of happy bodies,
the weather is warm indeed.

How we do it

Sometimes we snag on each other
a word that scrapes like a kitchen
grater, one *I forgot* too many, a joke
that leaves a purple bruise.

Sometimes we forget to see each
other. We pass without noticing
two trucks traveling in opposite
directions on a turnpike.

Sometimes we insist too much
banging a nail until it disappears
into soft wood. We are busy creatures
of error and haste.

But mostly we sail along on a sea
of cream; mostly we curve together
like parentheses with our love between,
mostly we knit tightly.

Mostly we make our marriage with care
patching, sealing any cracks, carting
in new furniture to replace the worn,
new pictures on the walls.

This is our peculiar house we've built
to outlast seasons and storms
as much a part of me as the shell
of a venturing snail.

Warm heart

You're always warm: warm hands
smooth back sleek as a Burmese cat.
Sunny weather outside and in.

When we met, I was frozen through.
My marriage of rocks and ice
had worn me to an icicle hanging

afraid to drop and shatter. You
thawed me. Every day you speak
of how you love me and I can

scarcely believe I've won this.
No one can *make* another happy
but still we can please, soothe

embrace. We can trudge along
my hand in your firm hand
until I am warmed by your sun.

Hairy nocturne

Come to bed as rain
crawls over the roof
fingers the windows.

Night is thick
as couch stuffing.
It thrusts our eyes full.

Neighbors have gone south
with robins and humming
birds. Foxes: our neighbors

this winter and coywolves,
great horned owls
fisher cats, predators

all whose supper we
hear scream. Come
to bed, pull the quilt

up over our warm

bodies and knit them
together, a silken

blanket of answered
wishes. We too eat
flesh. The fox no

longer fears us but
prances past, playing
with a dead mouse.

Let us blend into night
together—one large
heat-seeking missile.

What happiness looks like

Some things are ordinary but perfect:
drinking coffee on summer mornings
with you as the cats laze about, fed,
on you or on me or curled together
in the bay window on a sunny pillow.
Outside the weeping beech stirs
in the wind, leaves hanging down
like just washed long tresses.
We talk softly of the pending day.
This is all I would need of heaven
that I don't believe in, but this
I believe.

A litany of adoration

For all the mornings you make coffee
downstairs and bring it to me, for all
the times you make tea when I'm sick,
for all the times you drive me to doctors,
to shops, to readings and workshops,
for times you praise my face, for all
the times you love my aging body,
for your willingness decades ago
to learn to live with cats and make
them your own, for your learning
to garden when you'd never touched
a trowel, for your wit and your humor,
for the ten thousand times you've
made me laugh when I was sour
as an unripe persimmon, for your
patience with my encyclopedia
of complaints, for your ability
to charm even a bedbug or a rat,
for your strength so much greater
than my own, your ability to drive
all night safely, for your talents
diverse when mine are single arrows,
for all the above and fifty more joys
I praise you, I adore you, I need
you to the last of my dying breaths,
my long sought longest love.

A Jew in America Now

The nonbeliever prays on Shabbat

I can't accept a personal g-d
who interferes in lives, makes
the hometown team win, helps
find lost glasses, will cure
arthritis if I beg. My only

life is this one. Tikkun olam:
work is my daily prayer.
Yet I observe holidays.
They're meaningful to me,
precious. I've written

a haggadah I update each
Pesach, I do tashlich,
say Kaddish for my mother
and bubbah. Lighting
Shabbat candles I see

myself, one in a several
millenniums row of women
arching into prehistory.
Tales of the golem, Lilith,
wonder-working rabbis

live in my brain and body,
fertilize my writing,
stories my bubbah told me.
Like my mother, I curse
in Yiddish, always a Jew.

Holy, holy

I was never looking for a personal g-d
not even in my poor and spiky childhood.
I was always looking for the experience,
the knowledge, the sensation of holiness.

Something beyond my self. Not lightning
or the whirlwind but powerful and still
at once. I thought of strong light.
I thought of the burning bush, consuming

but never consumed. From time to time
usually but not always when writing
something would seize me, bear me
up and out of myself as in an eagle's

talons. I'd almost forget to breathe.
It was never for long. I'd return
shocked, my mind on fire, a rushing
in me, a coming together, clarity.

It happens less as I age. Perhaps
I can't bear too much of what burned
the trivial from me. Maybe once more
before death into that high bright place.

I'm not a shaman or religious scholar
but from time to time something power-
ful, barely endurable, takes hold of me
by the nape and shakes me clear.

Hannah tells me stories

You told me tales, half in Yiddish,
half in English thick and lumpy
as potato soup. Stories of golems,
magical rabbis who could fly, but

of your life before you escaped
the hatred, the hunger that turned
your belly to an angry dog with sharp
teeth, the pogroms that took your

best friend lying raped and cut open
in the street with her skirt flipped
over her face, you said little, almost
nothing. Zeydah had told my mother

some of it, thirdhand to me since
he had grown up in St. Petersburg
where his brother hid his religion
to dance ballet at the Mariinska.

You told me of your father the rabbi
of the little wooden shul in the Pale
of Settlement, how he forbade your
marriage and finally performed it

but not how he died stripped naked
lying shot in the ditch with all his
other children and the men and women
who came to worship with him. No,

you told me romantic tales of heroic
Jewish women saving their families,
of dybbuks and Lilith, of how to ward
off the evil eye and salve a wound

but never of how the Pinkertons
killed your husband, how you wed
finally another man you didn't love
to feed your eleven children. You

listened to soap operas while sewing
for money. You loved romance but life
gave you blood and bones that would
have burned your lips to speak.

The wanderings of Hannah

You were running from: pogroms,
your friend with her throat slit,
the house with the little your family
owned burning, a neighbor cut down,
his beard torn off, a baby discarded
in the road like a dead chicken.

You were running with: the man
from St. Petersburg who spoke
nine languages, the handsome
Jew who dressed like a prince
but who had a price on his head
from trying to kick out the czar.

You were leaving behind father
stetl rabbi with a wooden shul
the calf you'd raised, the friends
you shared secrets with. Decades
later they were all machinegunned
thrown still breathing into the soil.

You didn't have a notion what
you were running toward, goldeneh
medina full of tenements where
rats feasted, children coughed,

women sat late with bleeding fingers
making flowers for ladies' hats.

Your husband organized unions
fleeing Pinkertons from New York
to Philadelphia to Pittsburgh to
Cleveland where they got him.
You lived in a walkup with a store-
front shul and Black neighbors

you cooked medicine for. You,
your cat and your brightest girl
Ruth kept a kosher kitchen. You
listened to radio soap operas while
you embroidered for money, as if
your life wasn't drama enough.

In the Lodz ghetto

"Collaborator" was a dirty word
when I grew up along with quisling,
fink, snitch—one who betrayed,
joined the powers that control,
sold out to the enemy. But

in a deadly mess, more than
coerced, a misstep fatal, options
rarer than unicorns, how shall
we judge the Judenrat, elders
mostly, who ran the ghettos

to save German contact with
our dirty selves? Did they see
themselves as protectors? Did
they hope facilitating Nazi rule
would save them? [It didn't.]

An ethical swamp. In the Lodz
Ghetto where Jews were jammed
into crowded flats, fed little,
worked much, the Judenrat tried
to make normal, joining those

whose marriage would be sweet
perhaps but short. Resistance

made them nervous: we'll be
punished, shot, starved more.
Don't make trouble. Obey! Quiet!

Jews had so often survived
by acting meek, keeping eyes
lowered, it felt almost natural.
Did they make life a little easier
or just ease the way to murder?

Pretending to normality, business
as sort of usual, does that work
in the long run, trying to appease?
What is the cost of going along
while the world they knew died?

Holidays sweet and sour

There are holidays I detest:
the 4th with its firecrackers
keeping us awake, highways
and streets clogged. Best
to cower at home, trying
to soothe frightened cats.

New Year's Eve when all
the amateur drunks careen
down Route Six and roar
into trees on side roads.
If I'm not looking to hook
up, the parties are boring.

I like Pesach best: combines
history, spring, politics
and great food. I'm fond
of Thanksgiving with friends.
In childhood, it smoldered
into war and candied yams

neither of which I enjoyed.
I like to observe both solstices
and the anniversary of love
with lobsters and champagne.
I like to give parties on Derby
Day with many mint juleps.

Rosh haShonah and Yom
Kippur always move me.

Minor holidays, the New Year
of the Trees as winter wanes;
Chanukah when I cook
for a crowd; all birthdays.

I celebrate what touches me.
What doesn't, I try to ignore.

The New Year of the Trees

In the Diaspora we celebrate—
Jews in Argentina when the leaves
are falling; in New England when
snow chokes the ground; in
the Sonora Desert when cactus
blooms; in L.A. when perhaps
it may rain; in Scotland when
there's still little daylight.

Yet we understand that earth
is turning toward a fresh season
and carrying us with it. Even
if what grows is cactus or only
fungus, we rejoice in who we
are and how we have survived.

We open ourselves too

My birthday and Pesach are very close
together this year, so the swelling moon
brings hope of new life within as well
as to the garden, the woods, the fields.

Spring is late this year, but the moon
has stirred the crocus bulbs under
the crusted earth to awake and push
themselves into the air. I heard

geese honking high up as they
thrust through the darkening sky
to let's hope a pond free of ice.
When the full moon rises I'll

conduct the ritual with food I've
cooked all day and the sweet
wine and the dear faces of friends
around the table like so many moons.

Now the festival that used to begin
the year with the green moon calls
us to think about slavery, about
freedom, about struggle as the land

itself tries to shake off the snow
layered with ice and the birds put
on bright mating plumage and we
turn our faces toward new openings.

Let all who are hungry

Let us at Pesach consider hunger, how it
hollows the body, how it consumes
the mind, how it weakens, how finally
a person can think only of food.

The Pesach table is crammed with dishes
whose savor rises like an ancient
sacrifice. Who do we remember
as we eat. Let's call to mind those

who must choose between warmth
and food, between medicine and food,
between a winter coat and food,
who sacrifice themselves to feed

the young, the feeble, the sick.
Let's not forget them as we rise
who can't share with us tonight
although we open the door wide

for Eliyahu and Miriam but also
those who hunger, may they eat.

That book is closed

Every year on Yom Kippur
I speak the names of my dead,
I call them to mind so they swim
glints of silver fish around me.

Yet every year there are more,
schools of them. Some dim
as years pass, some never.
New ghosts join the gyre.

My mother comes first to me
but so many more swirl past.
I almost think I can reach them.
How foolish. Only their names

and prayers seem to feed them:
just ghosts I can never touch.

The double evening comes every year

The night I light the first Chanukah
candles I light my mother's yahrzeit:
one set of candles in the window,
the stubby candle for her in the tub
where it can burn safely all night.

It's consummately Jewish, this mix
of celebration and mourning, joy
and sorrow. I remember the night
we flew on standby to Florida.
My father turned off her ventilator

while we were in the air, so I never
got to say goodbye. So I say it
as I light the first two candles,
as I say Kaddish, goodbye, my only
mother, mamushka, mommalah.
The wound that never heals

the empty place like Eliyahu's
chair that nobody sits in. No
matter how many poems I write
that fissure of longing never closes.
Yet sometimes I feel you there

behind me as I cook your recipes,
sometimes as I brush my hair,
sometimes as I light the Shabbat
candles, sometimes as I look
in the mirror and see your face.

Shalom in my mouth like a kumquat,
bitter then sweet

Why do we pray all the time
about peace, shalom, shalom
when we've never known it?

Our land in Eretz Israel, always
contested, still is. Penned
into ghettos crowded as factory

animals in their stalls barely
wide enough to stand. Books
burnt. Then us. Auto-da-fé—

whose faith was tested? Even
when we thrust roots deep,
into nations, hatred seeks us.

Peace is that promise we dream—
the city on the hill shining golden
but maybe that's just the sun

setting that gilds it. Shalom
is hope, hope that breathes
through all our year's prayers.

Making peace is the only way
to know it. I wrap that hope
around me like a tallit.

They were praying

They were praying.
They were shot dead. Two sentences
that don't belong in the same breath.

It wasn't anything they said.
It wasn't anything they did.
It was their identity he was killing.

We're so easy to hate. Like slugs, taxes.
We're considered white now but not
by all. I remember when we weren't.

Dirty Jew, dirty Jew all through my childhood;
Aunt Kate, father's sister-in-law:
He was trying to jew me down.

Irish Catholic kids chased me on what
they called Good Friday. Forced to sing
Easter hymns, Christmas carols in school.

Mother curled over her Judaism
like a wound she must keep secret.
These years we tend to be out, even proud.

Now that could kill me.
Little Hitlers abound.
It's back. I'm glad I'm old.

A Jew in 2019

No matter how many generations
our forebears lived in a country
we are always seen by many
as those who can't belong:

the outsider on whom can hang
any mask of what's forbidden,
nasty, below contempt. Seen
at once as weak and dangerous

we can be attacked righteously,
hate as patriotic virtue, religious
entitlement. We think we're safe,
assimilated, at home, belonging.

Then we're killed just for something
invisible, nothing done or said
because of a mother's identity.
Once again look over your shoulders.

Once again lock your doors tight.
Stay quiet in public. Change your
name. Consider moving across
a border. Teach your children fear.

There Is a Season

At twilight it began

The sky has become a giant
fish whose scales are shedding
almost silver in the moonlight
falling, drifting down, eddying
till they slowly bury our world.

Now snow has shrouded
the moon, snuffed it out
and still flakes come, now
faster as if to abolish every
bump and protrusion,

to smooth everything white
and anonymous, no path,
no drive, no road, and soon
no car. The air itself has
shredded into flakes.

It feels as if this long quiet
storm wants to abolish
everything human and even
all of living nature smothered
in its cold thick blanket.

White with sharp talons

I saw a snowy owl once,
once only. At Logan Airport
in January I was sitting in a plane
stalled on a runway, fretting

and then I stared out
the dirty window and saw
him sitting in the dead
weeds. He had a thin

circlet of dark, a coronet
against the glisten of his
feathers. He was close
to the runway, gold eyes

half shut, his snowiness
on lightly thatched brown.
He was silence with wings—
a shining pure predator.

It was a visitation
from tundra and dream.
I could have prayed to him
so still, so strangely perfect.

I lie awake, mid-February

The wind is getting colder
and pushes at the house.
From the north it crawls over
the maps of Vermont and New

Hampshire, arrives with snow
in its beard. Moon is a hole
in the ice where shiny stars
dart and slip away. Never

will we catch their quiet
fire. The great horned owl
moves soundless through
the pines. Warm blood calls

to her. It's time to brood eggs.
Death of mice, skunks, voles
will all flow into them. Only
crows can frighten her off.

We all have something to fear
as air freezes to the sky, as
little birds drop from branches
as coywolves howl and hunt.

Early March thaw

Today the ground is bare. Naked.
I can see dirt, dead grass, tiny
shoots of crocus against the house.
I've been given back the world

at least till the cold slams back.
Chickadees, tree sparrows, finches
juncos rejoice, even tiny kinglets
who bear red and golden crowns.

Grey squirrels wake to leap
from branch to branch. Skunks
are abroad for the first time
in months, males driven by lust

to search out females in their snug
burrows. My brain has wakened
too. The land has emerged alive
from its white shroud. Earth

suggests it's something to plunge
my hands into like bread dough

I knead. Looks almost edible.
Far underneath worms are thawing.

My spine begins to glow like a sea
creature of the deep, but a weight
instead is lifted from me. Seeds
arrive in the mail, packets of hope.

Power to the people—or not

March came to Outer Cape Cod on hurricane force winds. Many pitch pines were blown down, huge bushy green bears blocking roads. Our neighbor's shingles are scattered around her house like weird wooden hail. Power lines slither across asphalt like sparking snakes. A stormy petrel was blown from way out to sea to First Encounter beach, dazed and wondering where the hell he is, awkward on the ground.

I lay awake, the wind roaring and throwing branches and boughs against the house. I was afraid the roof would blow off the sun porch because the translucent ribbed plastic roof was bouncing up and down shuddering with loud thwacks. Water leaked into the dining room from the skylights. The house shook.

Our power went out at dinnertime; the cable followed at seven. At midnight I paced unable to sleep in the din. No lights were visible anywhere in Wellfleet, my village. I learn all of Provincetown is dark as waves lap up Commercial Street, pouring into stores and houses. Our mutual utility Eversource sends phone messages that out here we all should expect to be without power for days.

> Without power vast darkness
> foxes hunt close by
> moon wind waves huge

O frabjous joy, the turkeys

Some people are afraid of them. Some
people find them aggressive, noisy.
Some don't think birds should be so big.
But the wild turkeys have come back.

You can see ancestral dinosaur
in them. Dramas abound. Some call
hens the gobbler's harem. But females
choose their winter mate; if another

stronger, handsomer comes strutting
they abandon one gobbler for another.
Single file up the drive and steps:
the wild turkeys have come back.

They left us for several years.
Construction drove them off and away.
We'd see them by a country road
but they were gone from our land.

It's been a hard winter here, a hard
scrabble year ahead, bills piled, I'm
buying my dentist a new Mercedes.
But shout out: wild turkeys are back.

How the full moon wakes you

The white cat is curled up in the sky
its cloudy tail drawn round its flanks.
Waking, it struts over the roofs singing
down chimneys, its claws clicking

on roof tiles that loosen and fall.
Now it runs along bare boughs of the oak.
Now it leaps to the beech and sharpens
its long yellow claws. Sparks fly out.

The moon is hungry and calls to be fed,
cries to come into the bedroom through
the skylight and crawl under the covers,
to curl up at your breast and purr.

The moon caterwauls on the back fence
saying I burn, I am hot as molten silver.
I am the dancer on the roof who wakes you.
Rise to me and I will melt you to silk dust.

I am the passion you have forgotten
in your long sleep, but now your bones glow
through your flesh, your eyes see in the dark.
On owl wings you will hunt through the night.

At the turning of the tide

The river has been swelling all morning.
Now it turns on itself, giving back
to the sea all that it stole.

A blue heron strides in the shallows
its beak a spear that impales a herring
driven by sex to thrust upstream.

No eggs from that one will float
and hatch. Muskrats splash and dive.
A red-winged blackbird lays claim

to its new home, perched on a cattail
while his mate eyes a neighbor
with flashy wing bars. Busy, every

one is in a hurry. Even the aspens
are mad to push their buds open.
Clouds scud over the narrow land

to sink into the sea. The sea gives
land and takes it away. I too am
restless to take charge of my life.

Praise this tree

The sugar maple looks fuzzy today
buds just partly open on the wood.
Soon it will be a hanging city
of green. Already I see someone

too fast for me to identify
building a nest in its crotch.
Turkeys roost at night on nearly
horizontal branches, like clocks

huge in a row. Its lush foliage
will hide a multitude, grey squirrels,
six or seven kinds of bird. A feral
cat we tamed used to sit up there.

Its shade protects us in scorching
heat. It asks only to lay off
the ax, some sunshine to make
sugar and occasional rain.

Shouldn't we try to give as much
and ask as little as Saint Maple.

Gardeners are devout gamblers

Planting seeds is a kind of prayer
that a late frost won't kill seedlings;
that enough rain but not too much
will come to us; that devouring

insects will lay off the plants,
diseases will pass them by.
Each seedling: hope embodied.
Each year some flourish, some

wither, some seeds never burst
their shells, some young plants
are eaten by rabbits or voles.
But still we harvest something.

One year, many tomatoes, peppers;
another, much cabbage, lettuce.
The weather gives, the weather
takes away and so do bugs.

We fertilize, water and weed but
nature decides what we get to eat.

It's all getting ripe

The zucchinis are ripening perfectly
and just long enough, although one
hid until it was large and I made
soup we ate. We picked black
currants and I'm turning them
into preserves and booze. Birds
are happy we took so little from
branches bowed low with berries.

I am pureeing the cooked patty pans:
in winter, served with curry and butter.
Some cukes are almost spiny.
Some are long and glossy. Tzatziki
tonight. The dill, cilantro, basil,
oregano, lovage, thyme, mint,
rosemary all grown high or wide.
My hands smell great. So does

the dining room where they're
drying. I have turned strawberries
into jam. Fifteen pounds of spinach
frozen. This is my true summer.
Sometimes I get tired. Friends
say, you can buy everything
at the supermarket. I know better.
This is my dirty paradise.

Degradation of the peach

Once upon a not that long ago
a peach was sweet and juicy.
You bit in happily and licked
tangy honey from your chin.

Now they are mealy. Sweet
as pillow stuffing. Designed
for shipping, not eating.
Tomatoes will soon be square

as children's blocks and taste
like them. You'll bounce
them off the kitchen floor.
Huge strawberries shipped

from California have no savor.
We are deprived of the pleasures
of ripe fruit. We are warned to eat
fruit but these are parodies.

Apples are red we're told but
live apples dress in russet, gold,
green, have bruises, maybe a worm hole
but sing their name as you taste.

Summer, bummer

If you live in woods, summer
belongs to bugs. We're warm
blooded food trucks.

Ants enter the house in swarms.
The kitchen offers spills, crumbs
but my computer?

Tiny jet-black beetles drown
in bathwater every morning,
get into my hair.

Ravenous mosquitoes light
on bare arms, legs, bore
through, drink deep.

Ticks crawl up my body
bearing any of six diseases:
they drill, dig in.

Out there a tiny Genghis
Khan is rallying his forces.
They will win.

Abundance is wonderful and then it isn't

Last night I dreamed that you brought home
ten puppies who burst in barking madly
peed all over every floor, knocked down
lamps, chased each other and two fought.

I know I am already overwhelmed: many
manuscripts to read and annotate, beans
to process and freeze, same with peppers,
eggplants to cook, tomatoes that must

be canned, frozen, dehydrated right now,
herbs to dry, herb vinegars steeping.
This is the life we chose but sometimes
in late summer I want to run away

to mountains where no crop grows;
to a desert where nothing is green.

Hottest summer on record

Unrelenting rain can be depressing
till you feel your mind suffocate
in furry mold. But long drought
terrifies me. Trees are browning

the leaves like flakes of tobacco.
The creek shows its bottom
mud crisscrossed with old china
cracks. I find dead fledglings

under the oak. The roses wither
from the top down. Grass
is burnt straw nothing can eat.
Every pond has margins wide

enough to drive a truck around.
The air is filthy with exhaust
and soggy with pollen. Even
the cats have hay fever. Fish

bloat belly up in lagoons,
streams too warm for them.
The sun beats on the sky
like a huge brass gong.

Another beautiful day the weather-
man gloats on TV. Yes, another
great day for fox kits, corn
and turtles to die of thirst.

A sea change

The wreck of a destroyer
from a war long over—as much
as wars ever end; now most
don't—lies under the ocean

resting on the semi-sandy
bottom, bones, I imagine,
stripped inside: implement of
destruction and the destroyed.

But the creatures of the sea
have transformed it into
a reef of many colors, crusted
with shells, anemones waving

their filmy fronds, fuchsia
golden, cerulean fish dart
through. It's colonized, painted,
turned from machine of death

into a little bright hill teeming
with life, a work of art and nature.
When we vanish from earth
we see what beauty will conquer.

Somehow, communication

Raccoons' faces look as if they
wore masks, so we think of them
as burglars. Indeed, they steal
birdfeeders and carry them off

into the woods where we find
them somewhat chewed. They
prowl at night looking for food
or mischief. Mating, they growl

and carry on like small steam
locomotives in the bushes. But
one year a bedraggled pregnant
female took to hanging around

during daytime by the front door.
We took pity and put out food.
She became a resident sleeping
under the porch. After she gave

birth, she brought two cubs
to us to feed. Her fur grew glossy,
her cubs thrived. One year a skunk
often followed us outside, never sprayed.

He seemed lonely and interested.
I'm used to cat and dog buddies
but when a wild one chooses me, I
feel strangely, wonderfully blessed.

An argument of crows

The crows are talking loudly
to each other, some on pitch pine,
some on white oak branches
stripped of all but a few brown rags.

They're having a heated discussion.
Then one flaps off and slowly several
follow. Finally there are just branches
swaying in a fitful wind. They've all

gone where the first one suggested.
Apparently he/she [I can't sex crows]
won the argument. They hash things
out: consensus is important to crows.

They form a good community, raising
their young and passing on culture
generation to generation, fighting
off owls, hawks, mourning their dead.

A woman found one injured, nursed it.
After she freed it, it returned every
few days, not to eat but to give her
trinkets or just hang out together.

In winter I feed when needed: deep
snow, ice, storms off the ocean. We
know and trust each other. Sometimes
they've sung arias just for me.

Visitors at dawn

Deer lived here before and now with us.
Summer people mind their nibbling
on bushes they had folks they hired
plant. I don't mind their chewing

rhododendron in the spring when
there's little to eat in the woods.
I forgive their hunger for their grace
gliding through the woods like warm

shadows, flicking white tails
when they flee. Fawns and yearlings
with their mother gaze at my bedroom
window as I and the cats stare back.

They hide here in hunting season
and come in the spring. Deer know
where the safe places are, better
than women who scurry through

dark streets. I have held them
injured and felt the life seep out.
They move like ballet dancers
among the birches and I smile.

We all live and die here

The plants are chatting
in their chemical language
how we've stuck an animal
body among them.

They don't object
wish it would hurry
and rot. Ashes too
we have given them
my mother burnt

against her wishes.
Wisteria rampant, avid
grows from her
conquering the hillside.

Plants find vegetarians
a joke, muttering
in pheromones, they don't
think we count. They
brood on poisons, spines.

We pull plants we think
superfluous or done.
The plants judge us.
Green grow our graves.

Things to do during a blizzard

We live in the country with well water

Fill the bathtub. Remove cat who fell
in and dry briskly with towel.
Fill every pot and pan in kitchen.
Try to cook with every surface
covered with containers of water.

Jack up heat. Remove clothing.
Check the TV for weather reports
and radar every fifteen minutes
until the power goes out.

Put clothes back on as room
begins to rapidly chill. Put on
more layers. Put on more layers
yet. Mummify self in quilts.

Play with cats. Comfort rescue
cat at window howling at blizzard.
Play with bored cats. Tell them
how bored you are so shut up.

Curse climate change. Flush
toilet with last bucket of water.
Make plans to move to Florida.
Remember how much you hate Florida.

Remind yourself of homeless people
and birds out in the storm. Read
last Sunday's papers. By candlelight
start that novel you bought last April.
Discover why you never got past page 20.

Read the labels on cans you're
opening for a cold supper.
Whimper, whine, keep watching
as the thermometer slides down.
Try to be happy you're alive so
far. Realize spring will never come.

December 31, night closes in

It's too cold to pause outside.
I worry for the birds. We're
the last feeder for them in half
a mile. One woman died; one

neighbor sold to summer people
for more money than I can
imagine; the other is getting
ready to sell. It's spooky now

in winter at the end of a winding
road. When I moved here we all
were year round, nobody was
rich. Most people fed birds.

At night the dark is thick. Eyes
burn green in our headlights.
There's just coywolves, friendly
foxes, grey and red squirrels,

our dependent birds and us,
four indoor cats and the moon's
skull staring over the pines.
In the distance the ocean roars.

Mishpocheh = Family

Hand-me-downs

Mother told me when I was little
that the small depression under
my nose and above my lips
was the fingerprint of an angel.

She said when a baby's curled
in the womb, it knows every
thing before and after, which
is why babies don't want

to be born. But the angel makes
us forget. Otherwise we'd never
willingly enter this chaos, this
maelstrom of trouble and pain.

We cried upon exiting that warm
safe place where all we need
was given us while we rocked,
richer than we'd ever be again.

I wonder what it was I knew
then—I wonder.

My mother, the Jewish witch

She knew about honey on a wound,
spider web to stanch the bleeding.

She knew about ginger to settle
a sour stomach, peppermint

to soothe, thyme tea for coughs,
witch hazel on bites. She made

compost when nobody did. Spoke
the language of cats and birds.

Butterflies lit on her while gardening.
Bees never stung her although

I saw her pick one up more
than once. Women came to her

kitchen to have palms read. She
would have been burnt as a witch.

Father never valued her knowledge.
He knew about machines and math,

poker and westerns, rye whiskey.
She knew about dreams. Yes,

she believed in bubeh maises:

the power of salt and metal

to ward off evil, that menses
could curdle wine fermenting.

Her hands could heal and strike.
Nobody's like her any longer.

Meeting Woody, she read him
like a book. *Marry him.* I did.

Her ashes lie in my garden's soil.
Her wisteria will conquer the world.

Get up and go

My parents were happiest
on car trips. My father loved
cars and no matter how little
we had, how we couldn't afford
a dentist or a doctor, no matter
how many only slightly shabby
castoffs from Aunt Ruth I wore,
every two years a new car.

On the road they'd sing songs
from their youth. My father
would tell the same jokes:
"That cemetery's so popular
people are dying to get in."
Mother would obediently
laugh. Mostly Westinghouse
sent him to repair machines—

steel and paper mills, foundries.
She and I were turned loose
free of task or purpose, free
of him to explore or loiter.
We were never otherwise
a happy family. Maybe we
all were just glad to escape
our house to anywhere else.

Her rack of fancy shoes

My mother was vain about her feet,
small, always sore. I can see her
soaking her feet in some smelly
combination of household products.

She had few dresses but many shoes,
samples she called them, bought cheap
at some specialty place. And where
did she manage to go in them? Once

she had danced but no more. They
traded dinners with other couples;
mostly the guys worked at Westing-
house with my father in the shop.

But the women got dressed up. It
was for most of them their only
chance to put on makeup, high
heels, a dress smelling faintly of dry

cleaning, scent from a bottle kept
dusted on their vanity. Mille fleurs
my mother had all my childhood.
I think it was my older brother's gift.

She loved to get fancy, reminding.
herself of long-past happy days

when she could dab hope behind
her ears and onto her wrists

and go laughing into a night
that surely would romance her.
She still imagined then some man
would whisk her into a rainbow.

Inside of me as once inside of her

Lovers from decades ago, I can't
conjure their faces with accuracy.
But my mother who died thirty
years past, her voice is still

caught in my ears like a fish
tangled in a weir. Her face
young, middle aged, old hangs
in my brain as if in a gallery

in a museum, her permanent
exhibit. Our mothers are part
of our flesh, our bones. We
carry them like a blessing

or curse all our days. I hear
myself shouting her profanity
exactly when I drop some object
on my foot or a zipper's stuck.

My life was as alien to her as if
I were a giraffe or a dolphin.
I've carried her into lands
she couldn't imagine, a love

she dreamed of till death closed
that door. My choices scared her.
My sex exploits shocked her.
Yet still she lives in my life.

Decades have passed

Mother, would you know me now?
You were jealous of my slenderness
always asked how I stayed thin.
I had no answer. And now I'm fleshy

not like you were, in your misery
only something sweet could quiet
but would you know me? Your eyes
are mine now, I ache as you did.

I can't any longer walk ten miles
on new titanic knees. I had
cataracts the same as you, but I
could pay to have them removed.

I don't have to beg to buy a new
coat. Watching your life, I swore
always to support myself and have
but poverty we shared shaped me.

I am always laying up food in case
it goes away. I have more sweaters
than I need. I buy in bulk and stow.
I will always fear indebtedness.

I like to think you'd look in my face
and still say daughter. I am only

a few years younger than you were
when I lost you, flying south

when my father turned off your
ventilator so I never said goodbye.
I dream you stand in my kitchen
watching me cook and you smile.

Without warning, a door

In the pit of the night, a door
in my mind opened and my mother
came through, not as she was
in her eighties, no, still vibrant,

flirty, her hair in a braid round
her head black as a crow's feather
wearing a summer dress turquoise
with white daisies, laughing loud

from her belly as never in those
last lonely years bumping around
the Florida house she hated without
women friends, just my father

to belittle and grump at her. How
vibrating with strength and energy
before disdain and lacklove wore her
to a fading nubbin of loose flesh.

How much can any woman endure
before she lets hope flitter off?
Before she watches death coming
and smiles as she used to, decades

before when she saw a handsome
man—he had to be handsome—
making eye contact and she knew
she could have him if she chose.

The patrilineal side

My father was a mantel wooden clock
with intricate busy insides although
all those cogs did nothing but tell
time like any digital watch.

My father was a snorting steam
engine eating coal and dirtying
the air. A self-castrated bull
with long shiny killing horns.

My father was a book of jokes
men laughed at and the women
put on simpering faces. A bottle
of Old Overcoat two thirds drunk.

My father was a face turned away
from me. A polar blast on my mother.
Shoes that had to be polished
till they shone like black agates.

He was a cold pew where I knelt
praying for love that never arrived.

Casualties

Some parents fight invisibly
as if children can't smell
the char of burnt love.

Some parents fight with glances
like the slash of a jeweled dagger
"dear," "darling" turned insults.

Some parents fight like tigers
defending each one's territory
almost to death, blood on the walls.

Some fight using their children
as weapons hurled back and
forth. These are the worst.

Why people include pets in their wills

Animals pass through our lives—
the cats, the dogs, the birds
even the poor painted turtles
from dime stores in my childhood—

some with a presence that fades
only slowly after they die, for
mostly they are with us a decade
perhaps, at most twenty years—

some we barely remember or not
at all. Fish in a tank have no
names or histories for us. But pets
who ate and watched and slept with us

are remembered as we do our exes
but with more tenderness. We gazed
into each other's eyes, we stroked,
we wept into their fur and found

comfort. They sopped up our
loneliness like broth into bread
and we told them secrets no human
was permitted ever to guess.

Afternoon of a housecat

The cat lies sprawled in a patch
of sun in the bay window, a little
bored but otherwise content.

She watches a small beige moth
looking for a meal. She considers
chasing it but she has caught many

moths and they are a mouthful
of dust. No flavor whatsoever.
Her tail twitches on the shelf not

with anger but indecision,
a state she finds uncomfortable.
She lets her eyelids slide down.

If she cannot see the moth, she
need not decide. The sun
is a mother who caresses her.

Once she was cold but now she
is warm; once she was hungry
and would have chased the moth

to have anything in her belly. Once

she slept on gravel and under bushes.
This all belongs to me, she thinks,

the woman, the man, the other cat
too young not to be stupid,
the dish that fills with food twice

a day, the daily cleaned litterbox,
the bed where she climbs after
the big ones sleep to find warmth.

All is good and she will spare
the moth because she doesn't need
it. She has everything she needs.

The rescue kitten

Thursday we will go with carrier,
a handful of treats and trepidation
to pick her out of a cage. Will
the other three cats accept her?

They will race through the rooms
of our house chasing, counting
coup. She will be part of our
lives for long years and years:

playful or a white pillow? Will
she curl with the others or sulk
alone? Will she love us? How
brave were women who walked

into marriage blind giving body
and fate to a man chosen by elders.
We will fetch the little one home
like a bag of tender groceries.

Feral no more

We rescued a skinny feral kitten
flea-ravaged with snotty nose,
three kinds of parasites, coat
ragged. You hid under a bed

for a month. Slowly I enticed
you out, changed your name
to Malkah, queen, first taught
you to play, then slowly

seduced you to petting. How
you grew, big and bigger,
longish soft coat of apricot
and snowy white, sweet face

with huge yellow eyes, a purr
that could be heard a room
away. You slept pressed
to my side and kneaded me

to sleep so many arid nights.
You were mostly silent, but
with body language could
communicate subtle desires

hunger, fears and protests. We
had only to meet your gaze

and you'd purr. You were wise
and tolerant of all the other

cats, would only quell them
with a stare if they misbehaved.
In your failing strength I saw
my future. In your growing

confusion, my worst fears. You
began in hunger, then comfort,
love and plenty; now you lie
under a blanket of soil and snow.

You're quite gone

At times the missing pricks me
a needle forgotten in a couch
cushion, drawing blood.

We had plans and plans, now
discarded like empty boxes;
dim sum, museums, flower shows.

We shared poetry and raunchy
jokes. My gay girlfriend, you
were more honest about sex

with me than others ever were.
We trusted ourselves vulnerable.
Too much reminds me of you.

I can't let go but have no choice.
The day you died, I scolded you
about taking on too much, begged

you to slow down. And then
words stopped. Now silence fills
the place you were there with me.

Sugar Ray slowly leaving

Sweet boy, you have for over seventeen years
been my purring shadow, my furry hot water
bottle, my companion through operations,
illness, troubles, hurricanes, blizzards.

You were always there. Now only one third here.
Mostly deaf, partly blind, eaten away by kidney
disease, your mind dissolving: we study dying
through our animals who leave us behind.

I hold you as much as I can and you still purr.
But you startle at coffee cups and a tossed
bathrobe. Fear is your waking companion.
You pee wherever you find yourself

then stare at me with mild surprise. Oh,
did I do that? I watch the end approaching
like an icy wind bringing frost from the pole
to take what's left of you from me.

Old photo: father

Among old family photos, one
of my father still young, leaning
on the hood of his black Model T

smiling wide as I never saw him
one hand splayed on the fender
as if it were the thigh of a girl.

What made him happy? A new
car, sure, beer sort of, rye whiskey
absolutely, poker, telling an off

color joke to his pals from work,
ice fishing in a shanty well stocked
with sandwiches and booze. Don't

mind the fish. He liked his meat
and potatoes. What could we give
him? Nothing he really wanted.

A Jewish wife he was ashamed of.
A daughter who didn't giggle or flirt.
Useless appendages he dragged along.

My dolls had more clothes than me

Grandma, Bubbeh, spent half the year
in our tiny house, sharing my bed.
I had one new doll and three cast
off by some other girl, now mine.

Hannah had cataracts sealing
her eyes. She'd embroidered
for a living bent over fine stitches
years after Zeydeh was killed.

She could see enough to judge
color. She took scraps from blouses,
tablecloths, dresses, sewed clothes
for my dolls, each with a wardrobe.

My dolls were better dressed than me.
She even made a frock for my cat
but he refused to wear it. I didn't
blame him for I had one good dress

of polka dot itchy cloth that scraped
my arms raw where it touched.
I'd have liked to have the clothes
Bubbeh made for myself.

She poured stories into my ears
at night when we weren't yet
asleep and they became me.
Stories were my childhood home.

Early education

My mother taught me how to can
and that was good; I put up paste
tomatoes whole and three kinds
of sauce, relish, preserves. My
storage room is beautiful.

My mother taught me I was ugly
and that was bad. As soon
as I left home, I could see how
men and some women looked
at me. I reveled in their wanting.

My mother taught me to garden
with compost and that was good.
We produce all our vegetables
except exotics like artichokes.
From our soil we grow healthy.

My mother tried to teach me to flirt.
It didn't take. I watched her
and turned away. I was blunt
as a brick. Somehow it worked
for me. I live inside love.

My mother taught me to protect
spiders, feed birds, speak
with cats and cherish them,

be alert and observe, and to
expect to enjoy sex and I do.

My mother wanted me to live
at home bringing back a pay
check from a typing job. I fled
to college on scholarship, came
back on brief visits, wrote books.

When we're children loved and
despised in equal measure, how
do we pick our way among rules,
curses, blessings; how make our
own truth from mistakes and lies?

The karma of heredity

One morning my mother's eyes stared
at me out of the bathroom mirror and no matter
how I wiped away the steam, her eyes
met what had always been mine.

Do I complain like my mother? My life
shines so much brighter than hers had
the chance. I am freer, could pick a new
coat or paint or lover or car I fancied.

Yet I hear her voice creep from my throat.
There she is curling inside my cells.
Her passed on genes model my aging.
I thought I could pick and choose

which parts of her to take inside, which
to reject, what I feared to become.

Acknowledgments

"Legacy of a vacant lot," *Muddy River Poetry Review,* online, April 2020.

"The air smelled dirty," *Third Wednesday.*

"Late to find me," *Bryant Literary Review,* vol. 19, 2018.

"Images in oil," *Chiron Review,* no. 107, Spring 2017.

"The afterlife of old desires," *The Poetry Porch,* Spring online issue, 2020.

"Save me," *Chiron Review,* no. 107, Spring 2017.

"At least a hill," *San Diego Poetry Annual,* 2016–2017.

"Night's siren call," *Patterson Literary Review,* no. 44, 2016–2017.

"The depth waits," *The Artful Dodge,* nos. 54 and 55, 2019.

"Even wine turns at last to vinegar," *Fifth Wednesday,* no. 20, Spring 2017.

"She is letting go now," *Patterson Literary Review,* no. 44, 2016–2017.

"Leftovers," *Poet Lore,* vol. 111, nos. 1–2 , Spring–Summer 2016.

"What goes faster every time I turn around," *Femspec,* vol. 14, no. 2, The Great Age Issue, Part I, 2013.

"The longest lesson," *Chiron Review,* no. 115, Spring 2019.

"Praise in spite of all," *LIPS,* Spring 2017.

"A good death?," *Hanging Loose,* Spring 2018.

"A profitable undeath," *X-PERI,* Spring 2016.

"A reckoning in flesh," *Knot Magazine,* Spring 2015.

"Joy to the world," *Mason Street Review,* 2019.

"Dirge for my country," *Monthly Review,* February 2017.

"Way late December 2016," *Paterson Literary Review,* 2019.

"Consider these but you won't," *Monthly Review,* June 2017.

"U.S.," *Meat for Tea,* 2019.

"Their mouths are closed," *San Diego Poetry Annual,* 2017–2018.

"How does it end?" *Monthly Review,* September 2018.

"Illegal with only hope," *San Diego Poetry Annual,* 2017–2018.

"Ladies who judge," *Northwestern University Press Anthology,* September 2019.

"Noon in a three-star restaurant," *Chiron Review,* no. 114, Winter 2018.

"The President speaks," *Nasty Women Poets,* Lost Horse Press, 2017.

"This is our legacy," *Monthly Review,* October 2019.

"Endless rage," *LIPS,* nos. 48–49, Spring 2018.

"Another request comes in," *The Poetry Porch,* Spring online issue, 2018.

"Charleston massacre," *Monthly Review,* vol. 67, no. 3, July–August 2015.

"Call to action," *LIPS,* nos. 48–49, 2016.

"Much too early marriage," *Paterson Literary Review,* 2017.

"French lessons," *Visions International,* 2019.

"Chicago one summer," *December,* vol. 28, no. 1, Spring–Summer 2017.

"Remnants of a dead marriage," *LIPS,* nos. 45–46, 2017.

"Fooled again, she said," *Muddy River Poetry Review,* Spring online issue, 2018.

"War of the old," *San Diego Poetry Annual,* 2019–2020.

"Where do pet names go in the end?," *San Diego Poetry Annual*, 2017–2018.

"The cemetery of spent passions," *The Comstock Review*, Fall–Winter, 2016.

"That wild rush," *LIPS*, nos. 45–46, 2017.

"No regrets," *LIPS*, nos. 48–49, 2018.

"Let me never count the ways," *Prairie Schooner*, vol. 83, no. 4, Summer 2010.

"In the end, only you," *Broadkill Review*, 2017.

"Fire in winter," *Poetry Porch*, Summer 2015.

"How we do it," *Paterson Literary Review*, no. 45, 2017–2018.

"Warm heart," *Paterson Literary Review*, no. 47, 2019.

"Hairy nocturne," *X-PERI*, Spring 2016.

"What happiness looks like," *Paterson Literary Review*, no. 45, 2017–2018.

"A litany of adoration," *Paterson Literary Review*, 2017.

"Holy, holy," Rose Rae's online zine.

"Hannah tells me stories," *December*, vol. 26, no. 2, Fall–Winter 2015.

"The wanderings of Hannah," *Paterson Literary Review*, 2017.

"In the Lodz ghetto," *New Voices Project*, 2018.

"The New Year of the Trees," *New Traditions*, no. 3, Summer 1986.

"Let all who are hungry," *Kerem*, no. 5775, 2014.

"The double evening comes every year," *Jewish Women's Annual Review*, 2016.

"Shalom in my mouth like a kumquat, bitter then sweet," *Jewish Poetry in the Third Millenium*, 2019.

"They were praying," *Raven Chronicle*, 2019.

"A Jew in 2019," *Moment Magazine*, 2019.

"White with sharp talons," *X-PERI*, 2016.

"I lie awake, mid-February," *The Artful Dodge,* nos. 54 and 55, 2019.

"Power to the people—or not," *Haibun Today,* Spring online issue, 2018.

"O frabjous joy, the turkeys," *Muddy River Poetry Review,* Spring online issue, 2018.

"How the full moon wakes you," *The '89 Lunar Calendar,* Lunar Press.

"At the turning of the tide," *Marsh Hawk Review,* Spring 2017.

"Praise this tree," *Muddy River Poetry Review,* no. 15, Fall 2016.

"Degradation of the peach," *Earth's Daughters,* no. 87.

"Summer, bummer," *Chiron Review,* no. 110, Winter 2017.

"Abundance is wonderful and then it isn't," *Third Wednesday,* vol. 10, no. 1, Winter 2017.

"Hottest summer on record," *Narrative Northeast,* 2017.

"An argument of crows," *Third Wednesday,* vol. 12, no. 1.

"Visitors at dawn," *Paterson Literary Review,* no. 44, 2016–2017.

"Things to do during a blizzard," *Mason Street Review,* December 21, 2019.

"December 31, night closes in," *Mason Street Review,* Winter issue.

"My mother, the Jewish witch," *Ibbetson Street,* no. 45, Spring–Summer 2019.

"Her rack of fancy shoes," *Rattapallax,* 2017.

"Inside of me as once inside of her," *Third Wednesday,* 2018.

"Decades have passed," *Poetry Porch,* May 2016.

"Without warning, a door," *Paterson Literary Review,* no. 45, 2017–2018.

"The patrilineal side," *Ibbetson Street,* no. 41, June 2017.

"Afternoon of a housecat," *Chiron Review,* no. 101, Fall 2015.

"The rescue kitten," *Chiron Review,* Spring 2020.

"You're quite gone," *San Diego Poetry Annual,* 2018–2019.

"Sugar Ray slowly leaving," *Chiron Review*, no. 115, Spring 2019.

"Early Education," *LIPS,* nos. 48–49, Spring 2018.

"The karma of heredity," *December,* vol. 25, no. 2, Fall–Winter 2014.

A NOTE ABOUT THE AUTHOR

Marge Piercy is the author of nineteen previous poetry collections, seventeen novels, a book of short stories, a memoir, a play, and five nonfiction books. Her work has been translated into twenty-three languages, and she has won many honors, including the Golden Rose, the oldest poetry award in the country. She lives on Cape Cod with her husband, Ira Wood, the novelist, community radio interviewer, and essayist, and four cats. She has given readings, lectures, or workshops at more than five hundred venues in the States and abroad.

A NOTE ON THE TYPE

The text of this book was set in Ehrhardt, a typeface based on the specimens of "Dutch" types found at the Ehrhardt foundry in Leipzig. The original design of the face was the work of Nicholas Kis, a Hungarian punch cutter known to have worked in Amsterdam from 1680 to 1689. The modern version of Ehrhardt was cut by the Monotype Corporation of London in 1937.

Composed by North Market Street Graphics,
Lancaster, Pennsylvania

Printed and bound by Friesens,
Altona, Canada

Designed by Soonyoung Kwon